First World War
and Army of Occupation
War Diary
France, Belgium and Germany

24 DIVISION
Divisional Troops
Divisional Cyclist Company
21 August 1915 - 18 May 1916

WO95/2197/2

The Naval & Military Press Ltd
www.nmarchive.com
Published in association with The National Archives

Published by

The Naval & Military Press Ltd

Unit 10 Ridgewood Industrial Park,

Uckfield, East Sussex,

TN22 5QE England

Tel: +44 (0) 1825 749494

www.naval-military-press.com

www.nmarchive.com

This diary has been reprinted in facsimile from the original. Any imperfections are inevitably reproduced and the quality may fall short of modern type and cartographic standards.

© **Crown Copyright**
Images reproduced by permission of The National Archives, London, England, 2015.

Contents

Document type	Place/Title	Date From	Date To
Heading	WO95/2197-2		
Heading	24th Division Divl Troops 24th Divl Cyclist Coy. Aug 1915-May 1916.		
Heading	24th Division 24th Divl: Cyclist Coy: Vol:I August to October 1915. May 16.		
War Diary	Perbright	21/08/1915	30/08/1915
War Diary	Southampton	30/08/1915	30/08/1915
War Diary	Le Havre	31/08/1915	31/08/1915
War Diary	Montreuil	01/09/1915	01/09/1915
War Diary	Bimont	01/09/1915	11/09/1915
War Diary	Lebiez	12/09/1915	22/09/1915
War Diary	Busnes	22/09/1915	24/09/1915
War Diary	Beuvry	25/09/1915	25/09/1915
War Diary	Vermelles	21/09/1915	27/09/1915
War Diary	Sailly-La-Bourse	28/09/1915	28/09/1915
War Diary	Bethune	29/09/1915	29/09/1915
War Diary	St. Hilaire	30/09/1915	03/10/1915
War Diary	Herzeele	04/10/1915	06/10/1915
War Diary	Reninghelst.	09/10/1915	11/10/1915
War Diary	Boeschepe	13/10/1915	28/10/1915
Operation(al) Order(s)	24th Division Order No. 9. Appendix 1.	20/09/1915	20/09/1915
Miscellaneous	Divisional General Order by Maj:- Gen. I.E. Capper C.B. Appendix 2.	09/10/1915	09/10/1915
Miscellaneous	Parade Orders for 24th Division. Appendix III.		
Heading	24th Division 24th Divl Cycl Coys Vol:2. Nov 15.		
War Diary	Boeschepe	02/11/1915	06/11/1915
War Diary	Dickebusch	06/11/1915	06/11/1915
War Diary	Boeschepe	08/11/1915	11/11/1915
War Diary	Dickebusch	11/11/1915	11/11/1915
War Diary	Boeschepe	11/11/1915	22/11/1915
War Diary	Hardifort	24/11/1915	24/11/1915
War Diary	Broxeele	25/11/1915	25/11/1915
War Diary	Tilques	29/11/1915	29/11/1915
Heading	24th Div: Cycl. Coys Vol : 3. 121/7928.		
War Diary	Tilques.	02/12/1915	02/12/1915
War Diary	Tilques.	01/12/1915	31/12/1915
Miscellaneous	Special Order of the Day. By Field-Marshal Sir J.D.P. French, G.C.B., O.M., G.C.V.O., K.C.M.G., Commander-In-Chief, British Army in the Field. Appendix IV.	18/12/1915	18/12/1915
Miscellaneous	Christmas Message from His Majesty The King. Appendix V.		
Heading	24th Divl: Cyclists Vol:4		
Heading	War Diary of 24 Divisional Cyclist Coy, From 1/1/16 to 31/1/16.		
War Diary	Tilques	02/01/1916	02/01/1916
War Diary	Hardifort	03/01/1916	03/01/1916
War Diary	Poperinghe	03/01/1916	14/01/1916
War Diary	Poperinghe	13/01/1916	31/01/1916
War Diary	Poperinghe	08/01/1916	12/01/1916

Heading	24th Cyclists Vol:5.		
War Diary	Poperinghe	01/02/1916	14/02/1916
War Diary	H.21.b.3.7 Sheet 28.	15/02/1916	16/02/1916
War Diary	H.13.d.9.2. Sheet 28.	20/02/1916	21/02/1916
War Diary	Poperinghe	22/02/1916	04/03/1916
War Diary	Appendix II.		
Heading	War Diary of 24th Divisional Cyclist Co. (B.E.F.) From March 6th 1916. Inclusive to March 31st 1916.		
War Diary	Poperinghe (G.19.d.2.9.) Sht 28.	06/03/1916	15/03/1916
War Diary	Poperinghe	15/03/1916	31/03/1916
War Diary		25/03/1916	25/03/1916
War Diary	Bailleul	02/04/1916	29/04/1916
War Diary	Renescure	30/04/1916	30/04/1916
Heading	War Diary of 24th Divl Cyclist Company from 1st May to 18th May 1916, inclusive. Vol 8.		
War Diary	Westbecourt St. Omer	01/05/1916	18/05/1916

Woodstock 2/12/12

24TH DIVISION
DIVL TROOPS

24TH DIVL CYCLIST COY.
AUG 1915 - MAY 1916.

121/7431

34th Division

34th Divl: Cyclist Coy:
Vol: I

August to October 1915.

May '16

Army Form C. 2118

WAR DIARY
or
INTELLIGENCE SUMMARY
(Erase heading not required.)

Instructions regarding War Diaries and Intelligence Summaries are contained in F. S. Regs., Part II. and the Staff Manual respectively. Title Pages will be prepared in manuscript.

Place	Date	Hour	Summary of Events and Information	Remarks and references to Appendices
Pirbright	21.8.15	7.30p	"The 23rd, 24th and 22nd Divisions will be prepared for embarkation in the order named".	WSJ.
Pirbright	25.8.15	6.10p	"Order of Embarkation of 24th Division" (Extract). Second Day 30th August from Southampton for HAVRE	WSJ.
			24th Divl. Cyclist Coy.	Q.MG2.
			Unit	Off:	Other Ranks	Horses	Vehicles				
							4-wh:	2-wh:			
			24th Divl. C.C.	8	198	4	3	1			
Pirbright	"	"	Train No. X 1010						From	To	Time
									Brookwood	Southampton	Starts Arrives Aug. 30 9.35 11.30 a.m.
			Extract from Coy Orders.								
PIRBRIGHT	20.8.15	12.30p	The Coy will parade in full marching order at 7.45 tomorrow morning - the 30th inst.								WSJ.

1875 W. W593/826 1,000,000 4/15 J.B.C. & A. A.D.S.S./Forms/C. 2118.

Army Form C. 2118

WAR DIARY
or
INTELLIGENCE SUMMARY
(Erase heading not required.)

Instructions regarding War Diaries and Intelligence Summaries are contained in F. S. Regs., Part II. and the Staff Manual respectively. Title Pages will be prepared in manuscript.

Place	Date	Hour	Summary of Events and Information	Remarks and references to Appendices
Aldershot	30/8/15	9.55a	Entrained for SOUTHAMPTON.	
Southampton	30/8/15	11.25a	Arrived at "	
SOUTHAMPTON	30/8/15	7.0 p	Sailed for LE HAVRE.	
LE HAVRE	31/8/15	7.0 a	Disembarked at LE HAVRE	
LE HAVRE	31/8/15	10.19 p	Entrained for MONTREUIL.	
MONTREUIL	1/9/15	11.20 a	Detrained at MONTREUIL and marched for BIMONT where Company is billeted	
BIMONT	1/9/15	6 h	Company billeted at BIMONT	
"	1/9/15		↓ Billets at BIMONT	
"	2/9/15		COMPANY training interrupted by rain, which has made the place very dirty.	

1875 Wt. W593/826 1,000,000 4/15 J.B.C. & A. A.D.S.S./Forms/C. 2118.

Army Form C. 2118

WAR DIARY or INTELLIGENCE SUMMARY

(Erase heading not required.)

Place	Date	Hour	Summary of Events and Information	Remarks and references to Appendices
BEAMONT	11.9.15	6 h	"The Divisional Cyclist Coy will move tomorrow (12th) from BEAMONT to LEBIEZ."	
LEBIEZ	12.9.15	3 p.m.	Company arrived at LEBIEZ. Billeted by Le Maire.	
LEBIEZ	13.9.15 to 20.9.15		Platoon and Company training, and field firing. Company Signallers trained separately.	C.S.S. C.S.S. See appendix I
LEBIEZ	20.9.15	4 p.m.	Orders received for move with remainder of Division. Platoon attached. A platoon was attached to each Bgde for preliminary roads & for liaison, remainder marching with y.3d J.B. No.1 platoon attached to y.1st Bde, No.2 to y.2d Bde, No.3 to y.3d J.B.	
LEBIEZ	21.9.15		The platoons named above reported to their respective Bdes. Remainder of coy detailed to march with Divisional Cavalry = A Sqdn Queens Own Royal Glasgow Yeomanry.	
LEBIEZ	22.9.15	4 p.m.	Remainder of coy bivouacked at LEBIEZ Ch. with Divisional Cavalry & commenced the march via TORCY – CRIQUY – FRUGES – LUGY – BEAUMETZ-LES-AIRE – LAIRES.	C.S.S.
LAIRES	22.9.15	12.30 a.m.	The Divisional mounted troops reached their billets at LAIRES.	
LAIRES	22.9.15 4.45 p.m.		Order received from D.H.Q. to detach five platoons respectively to y.1st & y.2d Brigades to reinforce platoons already attached. Three Bgades No.5 & y.1st Bde & No.6 to y.2d Bde. No.4 attached to y.3d Bde with No.3 to assist preparing roads.	Reference HAZEBROUCK 5A
LAIRES	22.9.15 7 p.m		Hd qrs of coy (all platoons being attached) commenced march behind 51st Cavalry Route FERVIN – WESTREHEM – AUCHY-AU-BOIS – ST-HILAIRE (which could not be entered till 10 p.m owing to passage of 21st Division marching South) – LIERES – BUSNES.	
BUSNES	22.9.15 11.15 p.m.		H.Q. & Nos 3, 4, 5, & 6 platoons commanded by Capt. N.V.H. Westropp, reached billets there at 11.45 p.m. from their brigades.	

Army Form C. 2118

WAR DIARY
or
INTELLIGENCE SUMMARY
(Erase heading not required.)

4

Instructions regarding War Diaries and Intelligence Summaries are contained in F.S. Regs., Part II. and the Staff Manual respectively. Title Pages will be prepared in manuscript.

Place	Date	Hour	Summary of Events and Information	Remarks and references to Appendices
BUSNES	24.9.15	7.30 p.m	The company picked roads for march of Division - routes (1) BUSNES - ROBECQ - MT BERNENCHON - VENDIN-LES-BETHUNE. (2) L'ECLEME - GONNEHEM - CHOCQUES - VEND IN-LES-BETHUNE.	Regt. Ref. HAZEBROUCK 5A.
BEUVRY	25.9.15	4 a.m.	By this hour all the company had concentrated at BEUVRY & gone into billets there.	
BEUVRY	25.9.15	11 a.m.	The Division moved via SAILLY-LA-BOURSE to VERMELLES, the company marching with Divisional Headquarters. Billeted in VERMELLES. During the night No 8391 Private Pearson was killed by shellfire in the billet. Matter was not gone into.	CSM. Reference
VERMELLES	26.9.15	12 noon	Orders received for company to proceed to LE RUTOIRE. Arrived there about 1 p.m. Employed in carrying ammunition, rations & water to 72nd Infantry Brigade trenches at LONE TREE. No casualties. Returned to billets in VERMELLES at 8 p.m.	Map Ref 35.B.3.4 36.C.
VERMELLES	27.9.15	3 a.m.	The company moved back to SAILLY-LA-BOURSE and remained there all day. Bivouacked for the night in a field adjoining BETHUNE ROAD. No 1 Platoon was employed carrying rations to ANNEQUIN units of 43rd Infantry Brigade from their winter trenches at ANNEQUIN.	
SAILLY-LA-BOURSE	28.9.15	5.30 p.m	Received orders to move. Nos 3,4 & 5 platoons piquetted roads for the division via NOEUX-LES-MINES - BETHUNE STATION - ANNEZIN - OBLINGHEM. Remainder of coy marched with Div. H.Q. troops.	CSM.
BETHUNE	29.9.15	3 a.m.	By 3 a.m. the whole coy. had concentrated and went into billets in BETHUNE.	
BETHUNE	29.9.15	2 p.m.	The company marched off via CHOCQUES - LILLERS - BOURECQ to ST. HILAIRE. Roads were bad & 6 p.m. breaks was delayed owing to roads being blocked with transport. Being the past four days the weather was very wet and cold, and the men were worn out with by night owing to the troops much discomfort and fatigue.	Reference HAZEBROUCK 5A.
ST. HILAIRE	30.9.15 & 1.10.15	—	Company remained in billets and spent the time cleaning up and overhauling gear & equipment.	
ST. HILAIRE	2.10.15	7 a.m.	Transport and billeting party moved off via WITTES to Batt. Artillery H.Q. at HAM-EN-ARTOIS. Remainder of coy stayed at ST. HILAIRE.	

1875 Wt. W593/826 1,000,000 4/15 J.B.C. & A. A.D.S.S./Forms/C. 2118.

WAR DIARY or INTELLIGENCE SUMMARY

Army Form C. 2118

(Erase heading not required.)

Instructions regarding War Diaries and Intelligence Summaries are contained in F. S. Regs., Part II. and the Staff Manual respectively. Title Pages will be prepared in manuscript.

Place	Date	Hour	Summary of Events and Information	Remarks and references to Appendices
ST. HILAIRE.	3/10/15	10 a.m.	The Company marched off to new concentration area. Route LAMBRES - KROMBT 1 miles g AIRE - RECQUES - 1st Eg STEENBECQUE - WALLON CAPPEL - OXELAERE - STEENVOORDE - WINNEZEELE - HERZEELE. Arrived coas at 3 p.m. and drew 2 pitched tents in a field. Transport arrived at 5 p.m.	CSY. Ref: HAZEBROUCK 5A.
HERZEELE.	4/10/15	12 m.	Extract from Bn? order. Detachments required from yr on 6th inst. 1 N.C.O. & 6 cyclists for permanent duty in Jnsdn. 3 o.r. to report to A.P.M. 5th Corps ABEELE at 10 a.m. Also 20 cyclists for provisions & report to Town Major POPERINGHE at 11 a.m.	Ref: HAZEBROUCK 5A.
HERZEELE	5/10/15	11.30 p.m.	Extract from Bn? order:— "Cyclist Company will march to RENINGHELST at 10 a.m. tomorrow."	
HERZEELE	6/10/15	8 a.m.	No. 5 platoon marched off to find detachments required, as stated in War Diary for 4/10/15/12 n.m. Remainder of Company marched off. Route HOUTKERQUE - POPERINGHE - RENINGHELST. Owing to bad state of roads and the process of lorries & transport the march was considerably delayed and the destination was not reached until 2.30 p.m. The 1 N.C.O. & 9 men billeted in a farm. Staff officers in tents. The Company formed a guard over the Divisional Bombing School and also over the Wood dump.	See Appendix 2 CSY.
RENINGHELST	9/10/15		Divisional General Order received & attached.	
RENINGHELST	10/10/15	7 p.m.	Extract from Divisional Order:— "The Div. Cyclist Coy. will march to BOESCHEPE tomorrow and take over any available pound."	
RENINGHELST	11/10/15	9 a.m.	The Company marched to BOESCHEPE via WESTOUTRE. On arrival the necessary billets were taken over from 2nd Divisional Train.	Adj: Ref: HAZEBROUCK 5A.
BOESCHEPE	13/10/15	5 p.m.	Extract from Bn? order:— "3 N.C.O.s & 9 men will report to A.P.M. for inclination clearing duties behind the firing line." Found by No. 1 Platoon.	CSY.
BOESCHEPE	14/10/15	4 p.m.	Extract from Bn? order:— 1 officer & 3 N.C.O.s will report to the Divisional Bombing School for a Short Course of instruction on Friday & Saturday mornings from 9 till 1. The G.O.C. wishes to bear Capts & Sgts talk consisting of 1 corporal, Lc. Cpl. & 7 men whose men are to be trained with the Cavd. Engrs task lodges in class B course of instruction with live bombs at the Divisional Bombing School.	CSY.

1875 Wt. W593/826 1,000,000 4/15 I.R.C. & A. A.D.S.S./Forms/C. 2118.

Army Form C. 2118

WAR DIARY
or
INTELLIGENCE SUMMARY
(Erase heading not required.)

Instructions regarding War Diaries and Intelligence Summaries are contained in F. S. Regs., Part II. and the Staff Manual respectively. Title Pages will be prepared in manuscript.

6

Place	Date	Hour	Summary of Events and Information	Remarks and references to Appendices
BOESCHEPE	15.10.15	3 a.m	The company was inspected by Major General G. I. Coffier C.B. Commanding 24th Division.	C.8.Y.
BOESCHEPE	15.10.15	9.p.m	Bal. order issued :- "1 officer 4 N.C.Os and 33 cyclists will report to A.P.M. 5th Corps H.Q. ABEELE at 11 a.m. tomorrow for permanent duty on control posts forbidden zone". This detachment, under 2nd Lieut CHAPMAN, consisted of No 4 platoon and the remainder of No 1 Platoon not required for clearing duties behind firing line. (see entry for 13.10.15. 6 p.m)	C.8.Y. Ref. H.S.B BROWN 5A.
BOESCHEPE	16.10.15	8 a.m	Extract from Bat. order :- Detail 4 cyclists to report to Q office at 10 a.m. for duty. They will be permanently attached to Q.B.W.H.Q. for rations and accommodation." Furnished by No. 2. Platoon.	C.8.Y.
BOESCHEPE	18.10.15	6.30 a m	Bn.t cyclist orders :- "G.O.C wishes you to arrange for 20 of your men to be training as quides and messengers by regional to any part of 24th Division area or trenches. You should obtain assistance of Divisional map sheets all officers under you should go out when men are trained & inculcate 'appendix'." 20 men of No. 2. platoon commenced this training under Lieut R.S. SMITH. The men from Nos. 3 & 6 platoons detailed for Bombing (see entry 14.10.15 page 5) commenced training under 2/Lieut P.S. St. GEORGE.	C.8.Y.
BOESCHEPE	19 & 20/10/15	p.m	1 Corporal & 2 men, reinforcements, arrived from Cyclist Training Centre HOUNSLOW.	C.8.Y.
BOESCHEPE	22.10.15		A digging party of 1 officer & 50 O.R, furnished by Nos 3 & 5 platoons, commenced work of digging in a route from a point 1 mile N.E. of DICKEBUSCH to a point ½ mile S. of YPRES.	C.8.Y. Ref. H.S.B.BROWN 3 A.
BOESCHEPE	23.10.15	8 p.m	1 Sergeant, 1 O.R, reinforcements, arrived from Cyclist Training Centre HOUNSLOW.	C.8.Y.
"	24.10.15	-	Parade Orders for 24th Division issued and attached as Appendix VII	C.8.Y. see appendix No VII
	28.10.15		Ann 2 Lieut D. man N.C.Os and men proceeded to RENINGHELST and were included in the Composite Battalion found by troops of 24th Division. This Battalion was inspected by His MAJESTY THE KING at 12 noon.	C.8.Y.

C.S. July for Major
View for Major G. W. of Cyclist Coy
Comdg 24th D. w. Cyclist Coy.

APPENDIX I.

Copy No. 6

24TH DIVISION ORDER NO.9.

24th Div.H.Q.
20-9-15.

1. The division will march tomorrow as per March Table attached. - It will be noticed that the destinations have been changed since the conference this morning, in accordance with orders received.

   The marches will be executed between the hours of 6.0 p.m. and 5.0 a.m.

   No troops will cross the LYS before 10 p.m. 21st instant.

2. Each column will reconnoitre its own route. A platoon of cyclists will be attached to each of the 71st and 72nd Inf.Bdes. for picquetting the roads etc. and for rations. The reminder of the Cyclist Coy.will march under orders of G.O.C.73rd Inf.Bde.

   The Officers commanding these three detachments will report to the Brigade Group Commander concerned at 10.0 a.m.on 21st for orders.

3. "A" Sqn.Q.O.R.G.Yeo.(less 1 officer and 15 O.R.attached to Div.H.Q.) will march under the order of the G.O.C.73rd Inf.Bde.

4. A rear party under an officer will be detailed by each column to pick up stragglers.

5. As other troops will probably be found billeted in the area through which the division is marching, billets will be very limited and troops may have to bivouac. In all cases troops and transport must be concealed by day as far as possible from aircraft.

6. The M.T.Ambulance wagons of Fd.Ambulances will follow up at a later hour their respective units, so as to rejoin them before 5.0 a.m.daily at the end of the march under directions to be issued to O.Cs.Fd.Ambulances by the G.O.C.the Brigade Area.

7. The 41st Sanitary Section and the Divl.Ambulance Workshop, A.S.C. (at present attached to 74th Fd.Amb.) will join the 73rd Fd.Amb.at LEBIEZ by noon on 21st Sept., and will remain attached under the orders of the O.C.73rd Fd.Amb.till further orders.

8. Div.Report Centre will close at the CHATEAU ROYON at 6.p.m.21st inst.and reopen at BOMY at the same time.

G.Stewart Lieut.Colonel,
General Staff,24th Division.

Issued at 7.45 p.m.

APPENDIX 2.

Divisional General Order.

9th Oct: 1915. Maj:-Gen: J.E.Capper C.B.

"The G.O.C. on taking over the command of the 24th Division wishes all ranks to know that he has been personally informed by the Army Commander that the attack made by the Division in the recent operations was very gallantly carried out.

It is fully realised by the Army Commander that the test to which the Division has been put has been a severe one. Heavy losses and considerable discomfort have been endured without a word of complaint being heard.

The G.O.C. congratulates the troops on this proof that they possess the proper soldierly spirit. He feels

APPENDIX 2

confident that all ranks will remember the glorious traditions of the Regiments and Corps to which they belong and that they will continue with cheerfulness to emulate the deeds of those who made these names so famous.

Much is expected of the Division and great is the work entrusted to it by our King and Country. It is for us to show our devotion by striving to be worthy of this trust at all times and in all places."

(Signed)
C. J. Stewart Lt. Col.
Gen: Staff
24th Divsn.

Issue

CONFIDENTIAL

APPENDIX III

1.

PARADE ORDERS FOR 24th DIVISION.

Reference Map, Sheet 28, $\frac{1}{40,000}$.

****

(1). A composite Battalion of men selected from the Division and from the 2nd Group, Heavy Artillery Reserve, will attend a ceremonial parade to be held at RENINGHELST on WEDNESDAY, October, 27th.

The Parade ground will be the filed south of RENINGHELST, the entrance to which is at G.34.d.7.3.

The Battalion will be commanded by the Divisional Commander.

(2). The Battalion will be composed of 6 companies each consisting of 1 Field Officer, 2 other Officers., and 80 O.R.

Companies will be composed as follows:-

Company.	Unit from which drawn.	Field Officers	Other Officers	Other Ranks.	Position of assembly and remarks.
1.	17th Infty Bde. (less 1 Batt".)	1	2	80.	Camp D.
2.	72nd Infty Bde.	1	2	80.	Camps F & G.
3.	73rd Infty Bde.	1	2	80.	Camps B & C.
4.	"A" Squadron Glasgow Yeo:			4.	Camp of "C" Btty. 109th Brigade G.35.d.53.
	24th Divl: Arty. (less D.A.C.)	1	2	76.	
5.	No: 2 Group, H.A.R.,	1	1	40.	
	Div: Ammn: Col:			10.	
	R.A.M.C., 24th Divn:		1	16.	At Camp of B.A.C. 106th Bde: G.35.a.10.4.
	41st San: Sec:			1.	
	36th Mob: Vet: Section.			1.	
	A.O.D., 24th Divn.			1.	
	Army Postal Service.			1.	
	Belgian Artillery. (No: 7 Regiment)	1		10.	
6.	Field Cos: R.E.,		1	14.	
	24th Div: Sig: Co:			6.	
	172nd Tunnelling Coy: R.E.,			8.	Camp E.M.4.b.10.7
	24th Divl: Train.			8.	
	24th Div: Cyclist Co. (without cycles)			4.	
	12th Sherwood Foresters			20.	
	1 Bn: 17th Infty: Bde.		1	20.	

2.

24th Int: Cycl: Coy.
Pet: 2

131/7693

24th Hussars

Nov. 15

WAR DIARY or INTELLIGENCE SUMMARY

Army Form C. 2118

Place	Date	Hour	Summary of Events and Information	Remarks and references to Appendices
BOESCHEPE	2.11.15	11.0.	3.O.R discharged from hospital returned, and taken on strength of the Company.	WJ
"	4.11.15	4.45am	The digging of the trench for cable (see entry 22.10.15) was completed. The party had been working at night owing to the hostility of shrapnel by day.	WJ
"	5.11.15	11.0am	A fire broke out in the building occupied by the Sergeants of the Company. The building was gutted and Rifles, & Rifles, 8 sets of Sergeants clothing + private property destroyed. Cause of fire is at present unknown.	WJ
"	5.11.15	1pm	4 Officers + 10 O.R. proceeded to PICKE BUSCH, remained territory billets there while engaged in work upon Communication. Remainder paraded + delayed two hours in consequence of fire detailed in above entry. Remainder party remains in BOESCHEPE in billets.	WJ
"	6.11.15	9am	10 O.R reported to Signal Office 24th Division to assist in filling head-quarters detailed in entry for 22.10.15.	WJ
"	6.11.15	1pm	2 Grenadiers from H.Q. returned for duty with the Company.	WJ
DICKEBUSCH	6.11.15	—	2/Lt P.I. ST. GEORGE placed in charge of certain defense works in G.H.Q. 2nd line	WJ
BOESCH.EPE	8.11.15	11pm	Order received for one senior N.C.O to report to Capt LOGAN R.E at 2pm at the WINDMILL DUMP RENINGHELST for instruction in duties as Jolly keeper at brickworks at POPERINGHE. (L-Sgt HOLMES)	WJ

1875 Wt. W593/826 1,000,000 4/15 I.B.C. & A. A.D.S.S./Forms/C. 2118.

WAR DIARY or INTELLIGENCE SUMMARY

Army Form C. 2118

Instructions regarding War Diaries and Intelligence Summaries are contained in F.S. Regs., Part II. and the Staff Manual respectively. Title Pages will be prepared in manuscript.

(Erase heading not required.)

8

Place	Date	Hour	Summary of Events and Information	Remarks and references to Appendices
BOESCHEPE	11.11.15	—	1 inf H.Q. MEAD proceeded to H.Q. 24th Division to be attached there general Staff to work on maps in connection with photographs taken from aeroplanes. Station now changed entirely. Nos 4645 Private ALLOWAY B.T. (wounded slightly - on duty) to hospital while returning to billets with working party. Nos 4645 Private ALLOWAY B.T. (severely) wounded, No 4594 R. Cpl. MEIKLE, E.T. wounded	Egy. Rof. HAZEBROUCK 5 A
BOESCHEPE	11.11.15	—	Order received from D.H.Q. to send 3 men detachment from DICKEBUSCH to eng H.Q.	
BOESCHEPE	12.11.15	5 p.m.	The men of the party for DICKEBUSCH were employed by this Coy of Divl Gas party has been working the weather has been wet & the trenches & paths deep by rather knee in many cases under water.	C.S.J.
BOESCHEPE	14.11.15		4 O.R. discharged from hospital, arrived from Base Camp & taken on strength	
BOESCHEPE	15.11.15	10 a.m.	Divl orders received: "All available personnel of 24th Divisional Cyclist Company will be attached to 2nd LEINSTER Regt for duty in trenches and rest camp. The attachment to commence on the 18th"	C.O.
BOESCHEPE	17.11.15	10.30 a.m.	Following message received from H.Q. 24th Divn:- "When party from LEINSTERS was fairly started to left & kind at BOESCHEPE to look after billets and any stores left behind." 9412 P.L. St GEORGE transferred to No 11 Stationary Hospital HAZEBROUCK. Sick. Divl order received "All enlisments of Cyclist Coy pay to 2/ Leinster Regt to be cancelled"	C.S.J.
BOESCHEPE	8.11.15	6 p.m.		
BOESCHEPE	18.11.15	11.40 a.m.	While the company was on a route march 4 hostile aeroplanes flew over & dropped 4 bombs in the vicinity of the coy 1 pilot on the W. of ABEELE. There were no casualties.	Ref. HAZEBROUCK 5 A

WAR DIARY or INTELLIGENCE SUMMARY

Army Form C. 2118

Place	Date	Hour	Summary of Events and Information	Remarks and references to Appendices
BOESCHEPE	19.11.15	11 a.m.	Extracts from Divisional order :— "Relief of 2/4 Division by 3rd Division. The 2/4 Division will join II Army Reserve..... 2nd Cyclist Coy will proceed roads from RENINGHELST to EECKE for march of Brigades on the nights 20th/21st and 22nd/23rd...... ROUTE MOTES — GODWAERSVELDE — STEENVOORDE Night 22nd/23rd. 2/4 Div. Cyclist Coy to billets vacated by 3rd Div. Cyclist Coy in J.5.	C.S.S. Ref. HAZEBROUCK 5A. REMARKS 2/4 Div. Cyc. to move into billets (less detachment previously at BECKE and HAZEBROUCK) before 4.45 pm
BOESCHEPE	20.11.15		Company picquetted roads from RENINGHELST to EECKE for march of 43rd 9.13.	
"	22.11.15	5 p.m.	1 Platoon picquetted roads from RENINGHELST to EECKE for march of 14th 9.13. All detachments (from ABEELE, POPERINGHE etc) were brought in to Coy. Hdqrs. The company marched to billets vacated by 3rd Divisional Cyclist Company at HARDIFORT, via GODWAERSVELDE — STEENVOORDE — OUDEZEELE, the platoon doing above duty following at midnight.	C.S.S. Ref. HAZEBROUCK 8A.
HARDIFORT	24.11.15	3 p.m.	The company marched from HARDIFORT, via WEIMAR — CAPPEL to BROXEELE where billets were occupied for the night.	
BROXEELE	25.11.15	2 p.m.	The company marched via WATTEN and SERQUES and was in billets at TILQUES, in the 2nd Divisional Rear area.	
TILQUES	29.11.15		Order from DIVISION. H.Q. "Detail 1 Officer, 1 N.C.O. & 10 men for police duty with A.P.M. at WATTEN."	Jt. Lt.
TILQUES	29.11.15		Order from D.H.Q. Send 1 Officer & 50 N.C.O.s & men as working party at DIVISIONAL TECHNICAL SCHOOL, TILQUES. every day till further orders.	Jt. Lt.

24. 5ni Gehringi
Vol: 3

7948/121

WAR DIARY or INTELLIGENCE SUMMARY

Army Form C. 2118

Place	Date	Hour	Summary of Events and Information	Remarks and references to Appendices
TILQUES.	2.12.15	9 A.M.	C.O. of the Company (Major W.A. Davis) admitted to hospital & transferred to No. 20 C.C.S. ST. OMER.	Ref. HAZEBROUCK 5a. 9f.
TILQUES.	1.12.15	—	Driver Robertson A.S.C. attached to their Company tried by Court Martial. Proceedings were adjourned till 5 P.M.	C.S.M.
TILQUES	8.12."		This period was spent in platoon and company trainings, the weather was bad and very little training was done, hindered to companies.	C.S.M.
TILQUES	14.12."		Extract from Divisional Order: "Lieut. C.F. YUELY Royal Irish Fusiliers to command 24th Divl. Cyclist Coy vice MAJOR DAVIS."	C.S.M.
TILQUES	15.12."		Driver ROBERTSON A.S.C. awarded by this company (tried by 4.9.C.M. found guilty) awarded sentence to 7 days Field Punishment No.1.	C.S.M.
TILQUES	16.12."		During the first part of the week company training was carried out but it was stopped during the latter part owing to the men being taken for fatigues at the Divisional School.	C.S.M.
TILQUES	20.12.15		Special Order of the Day received & attached as Appendix IV.	See app. IV
"	24.12.15		24th Division Order No. 28 received. "24th Division will relieve 49th Division..." by moving of Jan. 1st. Table VII(b) movements by Road. Date 29... 24th Divisional Cyclist Coy to WATOU via WATTEN. WEIMARS-CAPPEL — 200 function at T in HARDIFORT — WINNEZEELE.	Ref HAZEBROUCK 5A
"	25/26 Midnight		24th Division Order No. 28 cancelled	C.S.M.
"	26.12."		Christmas message from His Majesty the King received and attached as Appendix V.	See app. V
"	29.12."		LIEUT R.S. SMITH struck off strength of Coy. on Transfer to A.S.C./Under Royal Decr 21st 2/1 LECT. R.I. ST. GEORGE " " (invalided home).	C.S.M.
"	31.12.15	5.15 p.m	S.O. 29 received. 24th Division will relieve 14th Division Cyclist Coy will move on 2nd Jan. to relieve 14th Divisional Cyclist Coy. in its war billets at S4 9.19 d 29 on 3rd January. Route ST OMER — CLAIRMARAIS NORDPECNE — BARINGHOVE — OXELAERE — STEENVOORDE — POPERINGHE. The Coy will billet on the F at NORDPECNE 2/3 Jan. at HARDIFORT. On arrival in the new area 1 officer & 25 OR will be detailed to reconnoitre the 2/3 Divisional area by way of ZILLEBEKE SWITCH and to be prepared to act as Guides to all parts of the Divisional Area by noon the 6th Jan. An advanced party will be sent forward to reach the new area to take up(?) the 14th Divisional H.Q.	Ref. HAZEBROUCK 5A Sheet 28 C/9

Ch 1593. Wt. W593/826 1,000,000 4/15 J.B.C. & A. A.D.S.S./Forms/C. 2118.

APPENDIX IV

Special Order of the Day.

By Field-Marshal SIR J. D. P. FRENCH, G.C.B., O.M., G.C.V.O., K.C.M.G., Commander-in-Chief, British Army in the Field.

In relinquishing the command of the British Army in France I wish to express to the officers, non-commissioned officers and men, with whom I have been so closely associated during the last sixteen months, my heartfelt sorrow in parting with them before the campaign, in which we have been so long engaged together, has been brought to a victorious conclusion.

I have however, the firmest conviction that such a glorious ending to their splendid and heroic efforts is not far distant, and I shall watch their progress towards this final goal with intense interest, but in the most confident hope.

The success so far attained has been due to the indomitable spirit, dogged tenacity which knows no defeat, and the heroic courage so abundantly displayed by the rank and file of the splendid Army which it will ever remain the pride and glory of my life to have commanded during over sixteen months of incessant fighting.

Regulars and Territorials, Old Army and New Army have ever shown these magnificent qualities in equal degree.

From my heart I thank them all.

At this sad moment of parting my heart goes out to those who have received life-long injury from wounds, and I think with sorrow of that great and glorious host of my beloved comrades who have made the greatest sacrifice of all by laying down their lives for their country.

In saying good-bye to the British Army in France I ask them once again to accept this expression of my deepest gratitude and heartfelt devotion towards them, and my earnest good wishes for the glorious future which I feel to be assured.

[signature]

Field-Marshal,
Commanding-in-Chief, the British Army in France.

18th December, 1915.

1st Printing Co., R.E G.H.Q. 1973

APPENDIX V

Christmas Message from His Majesty The King.

The following message has been received :—

"Another Christmas finds all the resources of the Empire still engaged in War, and I desire to convey on my own behalf, and on behalf of the Queen, a heartfelt Christmas greeting and our good wishes for the New Year to all who, on Sea and Land, are upholding the honour of the British name. In the officers and men of my Navy, on whom the security of the Empire depends, I repose, in common with all my subjects, a trust that is absolute. On the officers and men of my Armies, whether now in France, in the East or in other fields, I rely with an equal faith, confident that their devotion, their valour and their self-sacrifice will, under God's guidance, lead to Victory and an honourable Peace. There are many of their comrades now, alas, in hospital and to these brave men, also, I desire, with the Queen, to express our deep gratitude and our earnest prayers for their recovery.

Officers and men of the Navy and Army, another year is drawing to a close, as it began, in toil, bloodshed and suffering; but, I rejoice to know that the goal to which you are striving draws nearer into sight.

MAY GOD BLESS YOU AND ALL YOUR UNDERTAKINGS."

GEORGE, R.I.

The following reply has been despatched :—

To :—HIS MAJESTY THE KING,
Buckingham Palace,
London.

The Army in France under my Command desires to be allowed to express its warmest thanks to Your Majesty and to Her Majesty the Queen for the gracious message received. On behalf of the troops I respectfully beg Your Majesties to accept the most heartfelt good wishes of all ranks for Xmas and the New Year and an expression of their firm and lasting determination to prove themselves worthy of the great trust which Your Majesty reposes in us.

From :—SIR DOUGLAS HAIG.

Christmas Day, 1915.

Confidential
War Diary
of
24. Divisional Scholar,

From 1/1/16

To 31/1/16

Army Form C. 2118

WAR DIARY
or
INTELLIGENCE SUMMARY
(Erase heading not required.)

Instructions regarding War Diaries and Intelligence Summaries are contained in F.S. Regs., Part II. and the Staff Manual respectively. Title Pages will be prepared in manuscript.

Place	Date	Hour	Summary of Events and Information	Remarks and references to Appendices
TILQUES	2.1.16	10 a.m.	The company marched off at 10 a.m. & proceeded via ST. OMER – CLAIRMARAIS – NORDPEENE – WIEMARS – CAPPEL to HARDIFORT, where billets were occupied for the night.	C.8.8.
HARDIFORT	3.1.16	9.30 a.m.	The company marched off at 9.30 a.m. & proceeded via STEENVOORDE – ABEELE – POPERINGHE and took over camp vacated by 14th Divisional Cyclist Company at 9.19. d.2.9. Map.28.	Ref. HAZEBROUCK 5A
POPERINGHE		6 p.m.	Order received from D.H.Q. 24th Division – "Under orders from 5th Corps you will provide the following:- 4 men to report to A.P.M. 5th Corps. ABEELE for Control Posts. Patrols from before 12 noon 4th to noon 5th inst. 1 Sgt. 4 Cpls. 32 Privates... Your Major POPERINGHE to report by 12 noon 4th inst. 1 Sgt. 1 Cpl. 15 Privates."	Sheet 28.
		4 p.m.	Order received from D.H.Q. 24th Division - "Detail 10 Cyclists for road control duty in new area to report to A.P.M. 14th Division RENINGHELST by noon 4th inst.	C.8.8.
POPERINGHE	4.1.16	10 a.m.	Detachments mentioned above in acks, for 3.1.16 paraded and marched off. They were found by Nos 2, 3 & 6 platoons. (See Entry for 31.12.15. p.10.)	C.8.8.
			2/Lt CHAPMAN & No 4 platoon commenced to reconnoitre the new area	C.8.8.
POPERINGHE	5.1.16	12 noon	2/Lt. LEAWOOD, Army Cyclist Corps, reported for duty from Army Cyclist Training Centre, SALISBURY PLAIN, & taken on strength of Coy.	C.8.8.
"	7.1.16		Capts. & C.S. WHITTUCK, Army Cyclist Corps, reported for duty from 3rd Army & taken on strength of coy.	
"	8.1.16	4 p.m.	Coy. in order received. Cyclist boy will provide Coy guides (infantry units) till 11th inst. 4/3rd Q.R. & LEINSTER, 2/3rd LONDONS, 6th BUFFS, 8th QUEENS, D.W.A.C., 8th NORTHANTS, 9th R. SUSSEX, 13th MIDDLESEX. Three guides were sent from No 4 platoon who have been known in the duties.	C.8.8. APR. 1
	10.1.16	11.30 a.m.	2nd Lieut. recorded Park of 3 N.C.O. in our beginners daily for six hours to report at H.Q. 24 A.I.V. at 9 A.M. to start to an officer of the Signal Company. Detachment provided by No 1 platoon & were placed in charge of Sgt. Robinson.	Rev.G.
	11.1.16		2 cyclists was detailed to the Division al School (5th Dvr Brigade)	A.V.G.
	14.1.16	9 a.m.	One man detailed to act as guide to R.A. Band to various camps in the Divisional area. He supplied to the Town that upon POPERINGHE.	A.V.G.

Army Form C. 2118

WAR DIARY
or
INTELLIGENCE SUMMARY
(Erase heading not required.)

Instructions regarding War Diaries and Intelligence Summaries are contained in F. S. Regs., Part II. and the Staff Manual respectively. Title Pages will be prepared in manuscript.

Place	Date	Hour	Summary of Events and Information	Remarks and references to Appendices
POPERINGHE	13.1.16	10.30 a.m.	Message received from 2nd D.H.Q. Capt Inch (O.C.) to report to G Office before 6 p.m. today.	B.T.G.
"	15.1.16	11.36 a.m.	Message received from D.H.Q. directing Lieut Inch to report to 2nd LEINSTER REGT at BELGIAN CHATEAU H23 for a short attachment. This was carried out.	B.T.G.
"	16.1.16	9.30 a.m.	A guard mounted consisting of 1 N.C.O. & 3 men — provided work full glasses to give warning in case of approach of hostile aircraft.	B.T.G.
		10 a.m.	Message from G trench for O.O. to report system of training for men still remaining with the Company. Also to report training of 25 guides for divisional area.	B.T.G.
	17.1.16	9.30 a.m.	30 N.C.O.s & men under 2nd Lt Slimming reported to Divisional School for fatigues. Sgt Major Evans granted a Commission in 14th Durham Light Infantry – 4611 Sgt C.W. Matthews appointed as Sgt Major.	B.T.G.
	18.1.16	9 a.m.	The 25 guides under 2nd Lt Chapman reported to 2nd Lt Leeworn for fatigues whilst training. They are to thoroughly reconnoitre the divisional area — particularly junctions & all approaches to the front line. 5 N.C.O. consisting of 30 men. 4 N.C.O. are occasionally asked for by the fatigue parties Grenade School.	billeted at Hrs 6, 3 & B.T.G.
	19.1.16		Men have been complaining of lice. A issue of Vermijelli's authorized used by ourarmy. The scarcity of cloths.	B.T.G.
	21.1.16	10 a.m.	A Field General Court Martial assembled at 106 Bde F.A. Ammunition Column for the trial of 9320 Pte Berry. 2 W – Pte Chapman persecuted. The case was dismissed.	B.T.G.

Army Form C. 2118

WAR DIARY or INTELLIGENCE SUMMARY

(Erase heading not required.)

Instructions regarding War Diaries and Intelligence Summaries are contained in F.S. Regs., Part II. and the Staff Manual respectively. Title Pages will be prepared in manuscript.

Place	Date	Hour	Summary of Events and Information	Remarks and references to Appendices
POPERINGHE	23/1/16	9 a.m.	Lieut. Lacky known returned from temporary attachment to Sherwood Foresters reported to 9th E. Surrey Regt to give advice on trench work.	BTG
"	24/1/16		All able to have been doing elegant out-work & so far as there have been no further complaints of tire. All the men still on duty have been taken for various fatigues & duties leaving only those necessary for camp upkeep	BTG
"	25/1/16	2 p.m.	A fine day, cold - considerable aerial activity. A German Taube aeroplane flew over our billets & dropped several bombs in our vicinity. It was heavily shelled & drove them by AA gun but finally escaped. No damage done.	BTG
"	27/1/16	4.30 p.m.	Lt. Chapman returned to the company from temporary attachment to 12th Sherwood Foresters where he was known as guide. He reported satisfactory progress.	BTG
"	29/1/16	1.30 p.m.	The weather has been very dull for the last few days & no heavy rain have fallen. It is still extremely muddy under foot. The 25 men being trained as bombers given relieved to the company from temporary attachment to the 12th Sherwood Foresters. Their officer will be relieved soon.	BTG
"	30/1/16	11 a.m.	The 13 men & 1 NCO working under the 24th Div Signal Co were today attached for rations & accommodation to the 13th Sherwood Foresters. Great attention is being paid to drainage of camps & drawing up hand orders limits to the order relating to any gas attacks which may happen. Inspection of camp by General Babbington cmdg 24th Div.	BTG
"	31/1/16	10 a.m. / 3 p.m.	It has been extremely muddy all day & cold but there has been very little rain lately & it is not so mud as underfoot. Men on detachment were inspected & deficiencies of clothing & kit noted.	BTG

APPENDIX 7

WAR DIARY
or
INTELLIGENCE SUMMARY
(Erase heading not required.)

Army Form C. 2118

Place	Date	Hour	Summary of Events and Information	Remarks and references to Appendices
			APPENDIX 1	
POPERINGHE	8.1.16		24th Divisional Order No 32.	
			The following measures will be taken in the event of an attack	
			i. —	
			II. —	
			III. —	
			IV. A Sqdn. P.O. Royal Glasgow Yeomanry atts 24th Divisional Cyclist Co. will join the brigade in Divisional Reserve & move with it	Mar 28
			V. —	
			VI. An Officer from each Inf Bde & Sqdn. P.O.R. Glasgow Yeomanry & 24th Divisional Cyclist Co. will report at Divisional Battle H.Q. as Liaison Officer	"M2 a.3.6
	13.1.16		Amendment (24th Div Order. G.713.)	"H16 z 1.1.
			The 24th Divisional Cyclist Co will move to R.E. Dumps"	
				B.V. Cramer
				Lieut
				in S.C.C.

24th Cyclists
vol: 5

WAR DIARY or INTELLIGENCE SUMMARY

Army Form C. 2118

Place	Date	Hour	Summary of Events and Information	Remarks and references to Appendices
POPERINGHE	1/2/16		The 25 guns to Divisional Area are being tested as to efficiency & give satisfaction. 3/Lt Chapman is proceeding with details to these men. The weather continues cold & foggy. There has been no aerial activity for some days.	B.V.G.
	3/2/16	3 p.m.	Lieut Juby returned to company after having assisted the 9th E. Surrey Regt.	B.V.G.
	5/2/16	9.30 a.m. to 5 p.m.	Capt Whitlock, Lieuts Gowdy, Sleeman & Heaton made a tour of the forward divisional area for instructional purposes. There was considerable artillery activity, the weather being fine was also aerial activity.	B.V.G.
"	7/2/16	5 p.m.	Message from B.H.Q. that Juby to report to 8th Buffs (six tunnels) for attachment. The weather continues fine but cold. Considerable aerial activity, several bombs were dropped by an enemy aeroplane in POPERINGHE. A fresh had has been put up in the camp for bicycle store.	See APPENDIX II "Camp" B.V.G.
"	9/2/16		A fine day, cold. Football matches are played as often as possible. There is no tidings B.V.G.	
"	10/2/16	10 a.m.	Continuous artillery fire was heard after early low and lasted until about 9 a.m. The artillery fire increased and several shells dropped in POPERINGHE	
		2 p.m.	Message from D.H.Q. received "Garalep" and stand to. He is so was fallen no writ gen	
		5.30 p.m.	Received another notice to any move were read on.	
		4.45 p.m.	Second German aeroplane sighted by sentry. Three bombs were dropped on the camp hut did not explode.	
		6 a.m.	Message from D.H.Q. "and 6 guns to D.H.Q. 4 guns to Reserve Anyere H.Q. (7 I.B.)."	
		7 a.m.	" " " Camel garalet stand to. Considerable artillery activity at night.	B.V.G.
"	13.2.16	9 a.m.	The bombs were recovered & examined by the R.F.C. The 14 guns returned from D.H.Q. and B.H.Q. They had not been used but were nearby. It officer stated the whole affair was attack on our left flank which was successful by the enemy. Heavy rain have fallen during the last two days.	B.V.G.

WAR DIARY
or
INTELLIGENCE SUMMARY

(Erase heading not required.)

Army Form C. 2118

Place	Date	Hour	Summary of Events and Information	Remarks and references to Appendices
POPERINGHE	14.2.16	7 p.m.	Message from D.H.Q. "Stand to." The company paraded in full marching order & all stores were packed up ready for a move.	B.V.G.
		9 p.m.	Message from D.H.Q. "Stand to" cancelled.	
H.21 & 3.7 Sheet 28	15.2.16	4 a.m.	Message from D.H.Q. "Stand to" & proceed to join the 1st Sherwood foresters at camp H.4 2 & 3.7. The move was carried out. There was considerable artillery during the night (Sheet 28)	B.V.G.
		9 a.m.	Verbal orders from Major Potts (D.H.Q.) to move into camp next the 5th Labor Battalion R.E.	B.V.G.
"	16.2.16	11 a.m.	Telephone message from D.H.Q. move into camp at Hulling Dump (H.13 a.9.3). The move was effected. Artillery activity h.a. decreased. The camp consists of huts	B.V.G.
H.13 a.9.2 Sheet 28	20.2.16	11.0 a.m.	The weather is fine & warm but cold. Considerable aerial activity in the morning. Message from D.H.Q. to Capt Whitcock. "Report here today for instruction. Instructions were delivered to train on our 35 gunners in the area of 6th Div. on our left - 50% of 1st battalion wrongly deferred the affair.	B.V.G.
"	3.12.16	11.30 a.m.	2 Lt Chapman with the 25 gunners started training in the new area this afternoon being made at BELGIAN CHATEAU. H.23 6.3.7 (Sheet 28)	
		12.15 a.m.	Order from D.H.Q. to move back to next camp G.19 d.2.9 (Sh.28). The move was effected.	B.V.G.
POPERINGHE	22.2.16 2-6.30 p.m.		Very heavy artillery activity heard.	B.V.G.
		11 a.m.	Capt Cunningham G.S.O 2. D.H.Q. gave bayonet attack instruction to leave all the available men to commence training at 34 D Bombing School G.19 a 7.5 (28).	
"	23.2.16	9 a.m.	All available 2nd Lt attended bombing school for instruction in 4 throwing & this hardly	
		6 p.m.	Enemy aeroplanes bombed POPERINGHE	B.V.G.

WAR DIARY or INTELLIGENCE SUMMARY

Army Form C. 2118

Place	Date	Hour	Summary of Events and Information	Remarks and references to Appendices
POPERINGHE	25.2.16	5 p.m.	It has snowed eventually during the last 3 days. Message received from the guide at BELGIAN CHATEAU* 4656 K9d 6am. struck by a piece of shell. He died soon after.	*Ref Sheet 15 B.T.G.
"	26.2.16		The company finished training on trench today. Received but completed spares onto populer road the mine. A thaw set in today. Wind changed from N.E. to S.W.	B.T.G
"	28.2.16	6 p.m.	Message from D.H.Q. "Gas Alert." All precautions taken. Every man at once slung on his gas helmet. Settled & came & went time always (airborne) to a previous D.R.O.	B.T.G
"	1.3.16	9.30 p.m	Message from D.H.Q. "Intent 5 men without cycles to treat L17 B20.(57) at 8.30 a.m. tomorrow. These to report to C.R.E. representative giving lorries from trench below to H54 a.9.9.(26) will be on duty all day. 5B. The named guide was instructed who worked well. They reported on their return that the lorries were struck by shell had to be turned back. They were used to convey bricks for "dugouts" at BELGIAN CHATEAU.	B.T.G
"	2.3.16	9 a.m.	Message from D.H.Q. "Gas Alert." Usual precaution taken. Message from D.11.9. for guide to open guide lorries from trench below Kelns near L17 B20 to H camps (Shenvoor Farm) A31 b29.(26)	B.T.G
"	3.3.16	9.15 a.m	From D.H.Q. "Men from 50 Div began messages received from minute of BLAUPORT from sheet 200 German prisoners coming down - more follow. German reinforcements were stopped by our artillery barrage. All attacks said to be successful on exfil - one small point which was being strafed and, or etc. Is was taken to the "BLUFF." It was later explained point at.	
		7 p.m.	*Guide to continue guiding lorries also a working party of 40 men were orders to lorries. She Shinning was ordered to be at back taken at 6.30 a.m. until 10 men on cts of	*Message from D.H.S.
	4.3.16	1.15 p.m	Message from D.14 @ Barrel Gas alert. Except gas & easily to clear in tomorrow.	B.T.G

APPENDIX II

Appendix II

Camp

The camp at G.9.d.2.9. (Sheet 28) is on the ground belonging to the farm. The barn in use for some of the men but accommodation being insufficient other shelters have been erected.

There are two "bungalows" — a framework of wooden props has been covered with straw securely thickly — a doorway at one end & two hinged windows makes an efficient shelter. It had been found advisable to surround hut of this unit a small trench on account of the wet. We have made beds by stretching wire across R.E. wire on the ground. These erections would be taken for haystacks from above.

Small "shantis" have been built of corrugated iron sheets, shelter tins from bent boxes, boards, turves etc. There are 5 of these & are nearly N.C.O.'s. The officers are in tents.

A small hut formed of wooden uprights & canvas across is in a cycle store.

A recreation hut in course of erection by the R.E. This will cannot actually of wood.

A washing place with washing basin & bench is arranged with canvas.

An incinerator was built — shells & bricks filled in with mud.

Gradually pathways were made of rubble with the proving unsuitable, trench boards secured from neighbouring good paths. These found necessary to have a system of drainage as the camp was a trench muddy.

B.V. Gowan? Lt

Army Form C. 2118

24. Cyclist
VOL 6

WAR DIARY
or
INTELLIGENCE SUMMARY
(Erase heading not required.)

Confidential

War Diary of 24th Divisional Cyclist Co. (B.E.F.)

from March 6th 1916 Inclusive.

to March 31st 1916

Bat.

Army Form C. 2118

WAR DIARY
or
INTELLIGENCE SUMMARY
(Erase heading not required.)

Instructions regarding War Diaries and Intelligence Summaries are contained in F. S. Regs., Part II. and the Staff Manual respectively. Title Pages will be prepared in manuscript.

Place	Date	Hour	Summary of Events and Information	Remarks and references to Appendices
POPERINGHE (G.9d.2.9)Sh28	6th -3-16	12.15 p	Message from D.H.Q. (Q2034) "Detail 5 men without rifles to meet lorries at L17 b 2.0 map 27 at 7.10am tomorrow to act as guides from brick kilns to H.15 d 4.3 map 28." These men are to continue guiding lorries carrying bricks to strengthen dug out. The weather has turned very wet & considerable amount of snow has fallen. The wind is prevailing in S.W.	A.V.G.
"	8th	9.55 am	3 from D.H.Q. (Q208 b) "Detail party to strike tent marquee at Bde. General Self today." This was done. Later The marquee to be re erected at postal refilling point by same party tomorrow at 10 a.m.	
		5 p.m	3 from D.H.Q. (G.612) "Gas Alert." Usual precaution undertaken. The wind had changed to N.E.	
		7 p.m	Order from D.H.Q. to the effect that working party 960 men assemble on night 9.9.4/10.th March to bury cables. The party will meet a Signal Officer at 6.10 p.m at H.18 d.8.4 (28) KRUISSTRAAT – YPRES RD. Work to be finished at 10 p.m (presumable).	A.V.G.
"	9th	9 a.m	Marquee party went out for erection of marquee. Its freezing today when is about 3°P snow. Proceeding wind N.E.	
		4.30 p	2/LTS SLIMMING & LEAWOOD and 60 men went out to bury cable at KRUISSTRAAT. Returned at 10 a.m. A.V.G.	
"	10d	10 a	Message from D.H.Q. for Corpl WHITTOCK to report there at once. He received order to select 24 intelligent men from this company to form observation pats on the front line. Also to report to brigade at DICKEBUSCH Dugouts for further instruction (17 I.B.)	
		1 p.m	Message from D.H.Q. (G.691) to the effect that arrangements are to be made for these observation pats to be manned as early as possible.	A.V.G.
"	11th		The detailing of the 24 men for the observation pats on the front line was is held over for a time on account ? Side much faxed in ? The Brigadier who controls these pats. Message from D.H.Q. "Head", "Please detail Lt SLIMMING to report to Town major POPERINGHE for liiteporary duty." 2 Lt SLIMMING reported there on morning of 13th. He awaits the Town major further arrival about today.	A.V.G.
"	13d		The snow has all gone & it is fine and sunny. Message from D.H.Q. (A2273) "20 men employed with town major POPERINGHE will rejoin this company on Wednesday 15th inst". Considerable aerial activity today.	A.V.G.

1875 W. W593/826 1,000,000 4/15 T.B.C. & A. A.D.S.S./Forms/C. 2118.

Army Form C. 2118

18.

WAR DIARY
or
INTELLIGENCE SUMMARY
(Erase heading not required.)

Instructions regarding War Diaries and Intelligence Summaries are contained in F.S. Regs., Part II. and the Staff Manual respectively. Title Pages will be prepared in manuscript.

Place	Date	Hour	Summary of Events and Information	Remarks and references to Appendices
POPERINGHE	15.3.16	12 noon	The Company is now doing Company training drill etc. 80 men employed under Lieut major POPERINGHE returned to the Company. They have been engaged in police duty. Theweather is fine & sunny, wind being from N.E.	B.T.G.
	17.3.16		Since we have been here we have armed an reinforcement. There has been no meet for there as we have been overstrength for some time. It is probable due to increases 9/3213 at the base.	B.T.G.
	19.3.16		The division is about to leave this area and move further south. The weather has been fine warm & sunny up to now. Message from D.H.Q. "Gas Alert". Later Gas alert cancelled.	B.T.G.
	21.3.16	9.50 a.m.	Message from D.H.Q. "Gas Alert". Message from Signal OC Sgt Hinton. Party of 9 men all 8 time return this evening. Many trucks to return, they have gone excellent very good work done. This party arrived back in camp at 3 p.m. They have been trying cables through YPRES S. The Officer of the Company went out today to reconnoitre our new divisional area.	B.T.G.
	23.3.16		Message from Q. D.H.Q. (A3071) to the effect that one platoon & Officer must report to Camp Commandant 24th Division in the new area and a view to taking over the new divisional area shewing Officers guard. Their work to be controlled by D.H.Q. Weather is now warm & mild.	B.T.G.
	24.3.16	12.30 p.m.	2Lt R.R. LEAWOOD and 29 men (given meal before) left camp to learn the new area under D.H.Q. They are to be attached to D.H.Q. for rations etc. Some rain has fallen today, & it is cold.	

WAR DIARY or INTELLIGENCE SUMMARY

Army Form C. 2118

19

Place	Date	Hour	Summary of Events and Information	Remarks and references to Appendices
POPERINGHE	25.3.16		24 D.O.R. read "The 24th Division will relieve the 1st Canadian Division in the trenches between March 23rd & 31st. .... & further orders will be issued regarding reliefs by 24th Division mounted troops -----	B.T.G.
"	26.3.16		The following G386/5 was received from D.H.Q.:- "The colour & pattern of the rocket which is to be used as a supplementary S.O.S. Signal ---- will in future be 3 reversible (asteroid) fired in quick succession ----." The supplementary S.O.S. signal will in charge by one red asteroid rocket, to be repeated until acknowledged. The change to date from 12 midnight April 2.	
	Later		Lieut Pritchard Amorin (G.183) has been received from D.H.Q. to the effect that the company will carry out a reconnaissance of the roads of the new divisional area. Reports sent in to indicate the suitability of various roads for different kinds of traffic.	B.T.G.
"	27.3.16	8.30 a.m.	The road reconnaissance was commenced with Lt. TUELY. The company was divided into groups under sergeants. The groups were divided into section under N.C.O.s Each section had 3 or more again to reconnoitre. The sergeants prepared rough forms to send the state of roads from the report of this section. Rearranged symbols were used to denote the state of roads. The group sergeants handed in their rough to 2Lt GANDER who prepared a rough on a large scale for D.H.Q. This work took several days to complete.	B.T.G.
"	28.3.16 to 10.1.16		Div Order (G.23) Divisional mounted troops to take over from 1st Canadian Mtd troops on the 30th and move to new camp on 31st midnight.	

1875 Wt. W593/826 1,000,000 4/15 T.R.C. & A. A.D.S.S./Forms/C. 2118.

WAR DIARY or INTELLIGENCE SUMMARY

Army Form C. 2118

20

Place	Date	Hour	Summary of Events and Information	Remarks and references to Appendices
POPERINGHE	30/3/16		The road reconnaissance of the new divisional area was completed today & report sent to D.H.Q. Lce Sgt White and 8.O.R and Cpl Fuller and 3 O.R. were sent to relieve Canadian 1st Division troops at S.53 a.9.9 & N 32 b.22 (28) respectively. Their duties being to act as trench wardens on sector of G.H.Q. 3rd line i.e. to keep it in a good state of repair. This relief extends from W.24 central to N 35 c.0.7. 2Lt B.V. GANDER in charge of 20 O.R.m taken over from Canadian Cyclist Co. B.T.B.	
"	31/3/16	2 p.m.	The company moved to new Campsite. S 22 E a 7.4. B.T.B	

WAR DIARY or INTELLIGENCE SUMMARY

APPENDIX III

Place	Date	Hour	Summary of Events and Information	Remarks and references to Appendices
	25.3.16		APPENDIX III

A proposal put forward by the commander of the 2nd Cavalry Division has been received here. It suggests that divisional mounted troops (Cavalry regiments) should leave their division & undergo a special course of training as divisional mounted troops. Period of training not to exceed 2 weeks & not to be controlled by the commander of the 2nd Cavalry Division in the neighbourhood of the area of 2nd Army Reserve Southern portion (QUELMES). I suggest two months might be taken over division at a time — their Artillery &c. unit the division for the time being replaced by divisional mounted troops of other divisions who in their turn would be relieved when they went for training. Suggestion concerns the 2nd Army only. I have been approached by the 5th Corps to offer the following decision made for its corps (5th): — | |

DIVISION	MARCH & AREA	DURATION OF COURSE	RETURN MARCH
3rd	TUESDAY APRIL 2nd & WEDNESDAY 12th	THURS APR 13th to WED " 26	THURS APR 27 & FRI " 28
34th	SAT APR 29 & SUN " 30th	MON MAY 1st to SUN MAY 14th	MON MAY 15th & TUES " 16th
50th	MON MAY 15 & TUES " 16	WED MAY 17 to TUES MAY 30th	WED MAY 31st & THURS JUNE 1st

Army Form C. 2118

WAR DIARY
or
INTELLIGENCE SUMMARY
(Erase heading not required.)

Instructions regarding War Diaries and Intelligence Summaries are contained in F.S. Regs., Part II. and the Staff Manual respectively. Title Pages will be prepared in manuscript.

20 24 Cyclist Coy Vol 7

Place	Date	Hour	Summary of Events and Information	Remarks and references to Appendices
BAILLEUL	2.4.16	6 p.m.	A party, 50 strong, paraded under Lt TULLY & proceeded to N.33.d.4.1. (BUS FARM) to work on digging in cable for 42nd I.B. Under instruction from H.Q. 24th Division this works to be carried on until further notice.	Sheet 28 C.24.
"	5.4.16		A party, 20 strong, is to report daily at the 24th Divisional School at 9.30 a.m. for work. In continuance of this the working party burying cables was reduced to 30.	C.24.
"	8.4.16		The platoon (No 4) billeted at 24th Divisional School, who have been busied in studies, returned to the Company.	C.24.
"	10.4.16	2 noon	2/Lt GANDER, 1 N.C.O. & 9 men proceeded to Frontier Control duty, in relief of 3rd Divisional Cyclist Company.	C.24.
"	11.4.16	10 a.m.	A party of 30 O.R. under Lieut TULLY proceeded to the 42nd Bde. Grenade School at M.36.b.2.8. to be accompanied there for work on digging in cables in the neighbourhood of WULVERGHEM (right sector 42nd I.B. area).	Sheet 28 C.24.
"	12.4.16	6 p.m.	2/Lt SKINNING, received from and relieving him Major POPERINGHE, having to TULLY in command of detachment at M.36.b.2.8.	C.24. Sheet 28.
"	15.4.16		The (re)party of 1 N.C.O. & 8 O.R. and 1 N.C.O. & 3 O.R. acting as Guard working, rejoined the Company today. 3 men (relieving) from D.H.Q. & 6 men for But Sqdn Coy. rejoined the company today.	C.24.
"	20.4.16		23 O.R. from Frontier Control work rejoined the Company.	
"	22.4.16		The Coy. carried out a tactical exercise in the vicinity of NEUF BERQUIN.	C.24.
"	23.4.16		7 O.R. from Frontier Control Duty rejoined Company.	

1875 Wt. W593/826 1,000,000 4/15 I.B.C. & A. A.D.S.S./Forms/C. 2118.

WAR DIARY
or
INTELLIGENCE SUMMARY
(Erase heading not required.)

Army Form C. 2118

Place	Date	Hour	Summary of Events and Information	Remarks and references to Appendices
BAILLEUL	24.4.16.		The company carried out a Tactical Exercise near STRAZEELE. 4 O.R. returned to the Coy. from Furniture Control Duty & 3 O.R. rejoined from duty as orderlies at 24th Divisional School.	CW.
BAILLEUL	26.4.16.	11.30 a.m.	The company was inspected, together with the Divisional Cavalry, by the G.O.C. 24th Division Major-General J.E. CAPPER C.B. prior to proceeding for special training with 2nd Cavalry Division.	CW.
"	29.4.16.	10 a.m.	The Coy and the Divisional Cavalry marched off at 10 a.m. Route BAILLEUL — STRAZEELE — HAZEBROUCK — EBBLINGHEM — RENESCURE, going into billets at the latter place. The column was inspected by the G.O.C. 24th Division while marching through Carrefour at HAZEBROUCK.	CW. Ref. H.42.E.B.Route Sh.
RENESCURE	30.4.16.		The Divisional Mounted Troops marched from RENESCURE via ARQUES — LONGPON WINS — WIZERNES — SETQUES — LUMBRES — ACQUIN — WESTBECOURT and VAL D'ACQUIN where the company and the Divisional Cavalry went into billets respectively for training.	Ref. H42.E.B.Route Sh. CW.

Vol 8
24 Div cyclo

Army Form C. 2118

WAR DIARY
or
INTELLIGENCE SUMMARY
(Erase heading not required.)

CONFIDENTIAL.

WAR DIARY OF
24th DIVL: Cyclist Company
from 1st May. to 18th May. 1916, inclusive.

May

Original

Army Form C. 2118

WAR DIARY
or
INTELLIGENCE SUMMARY
(Erase heading not required.)

Instructions regarding War Diaries and Intelligence Summaries are contained in F.S. Regs., Part II. and the Staff Manual respectively. Title Pages will be prepared in manuscript.

Place	Date	Hour	Summary of Events and Information	Remarks and references to Appendices
NESTBECOURT ST. OMER	May 1st		The Company commenced training today with the 24.t Divisional Cavalry. The advanced guard was practiced. All N CO's & Officers received instruction on the use & carrying with cyclists in the advanced guard. "Squads" were formed in which a platoon of cyclists worked with a troop of cavalry. The same platoon formed the one "syndicate" throughout the training. The main work of today was attention mainly aimed at by advancing separately when together. The cavalry afraid to keep for flanking movements (minor) cross country work, and in general where cyclists cannot proceed. B.T.G	
"	2nd		The same training was proceeded with as yesterday but the time was put into practice B.T.G	
"	3rd		The advance on parallel roads was practiced – advances were made by bounds. Tactical communication made of each bound. All men of the company were engaged. The enemy were represented by two platoons of cyclists. An example was given today of the use of cavalry. Cyclists were unable to attack a position & no cavalry was attached. B.T.G	
"	4		The flank guard was practiced today. As the country was hilly, cavalry patrols were used. B.T.G	
"	5d		Rear Guard action. The cavalry in this case retired but of all as it was argued that they are more suitable. B.T.G	
"	6d		Advanced Guard again practiced. B.T.G	

WAR DIARY
or
INTELLIGENCE SUMMARY
(Erase heading not required.)

Army Form C. 2118

Instructions regarding War Diaries and Intelligence Summaries are contained in F. S. Regs., Part II. and the Staff Manual respectively. Title Pages will be prepared in manuscript.

Place	Date	Hour	Summary of Events and Information	Remarks and references to Appendices
HESTRECOURT STOMER	MAY 8th		A staff ride for Officers took place today in which the country was suitability for outposts was discussed. B.V.G.	
	9th		The attack on a village was practised. B.V.G.	
	10th		The rear guard retire on S. wast was repeated move through B.V.G.	
	11th		In conjunction with Cav. Cyclists of 2nd Division Rearguard and advanced guard practice.	ret.
	12th		Advance guard again practised.	ret.
	13th		Line of observation thrown out ahead of Infantry outposts practised.	ret.
	15th		Return march halted at RENESCURE for night.	ret.
	16th		Return march continued to billets E. of BAILLEUL.	ret.
	17th		100 men and 1 Officer for digging party at AIRCRAFT FARM.	ret.
	18th		Company moved to billets near FLETRE to join 5th Corps Cyclist Battalion.	ret. RRC

www.ingramcontent.com/pod-product-compliance
Lightning Source LLC
Chambersburg PA
CBHW082358170426
43191CB00048B/2063